HANUMAN

THE IMMORTAL MONKEY GOD

Design for Children

Guru Gaurav Arya

ISBN- 978-81-968214-8-7

Dedication

To Lord Hanuman,

The embodiment of unwavering devotion,

The symbol of boundless strength,

The epitome of selfless service,

You who inspire us to rise above our limitations,

You who teach us the power of faith,

You who guide us through life's trials and tribulations,

With profound gratitude and deep reverence,

This book is dedicated to you, Hanuman,

May your divine presence illuminate our path,

May your blessings be our constant source of inspiration,

Jai Hanuman!

Contents

Preface

In the heart of Hindu mythology, amidst the pages of ancient epics and legends, stands a figure of unmatched devotion, boundless strength, and unwavering loyalty—the mighty Hanuman, the Immortal Monkey God. For generations, his tale has been told and retold, passing down the essence of his divine character from one storyteller to another.

As we embark on this journey through the pages of "Hanuman: The Immortal Monkey God," we find ourselves entering a world where gods walk among mortals, where the line between the human and the divine blurs, and where the boundless power of devotion can move mountains, quite literally.

This book seeks to illuminate the life and adventures of Lord Hanuman, a deity who transcends the confines of religion, touching the hearts of millions with his unshakable faith, unparalleled courage, and limitless compassion. Within these chapters, you will discover the timeless stories of his incredible feats, from leaping across the mighty ocean to lifting a mountain, all in the service of his beloved Lord Rama.

But Hanuman's tale is more than just a collection of heroic exploits; it is a profound exploration of the human spirit and its capacity for devotion, sacrifice, and selfless love. His unwavering dedication to dharma (righteousness) and his undying loyalty to his Lord have made him a symbol of hope, strength, and inspiration for countless souls.

As we delve into the various facets of Hanuman's life and character, we invite you to contemplate the deeper meanings and universal lessons embedded in his story. Through the ages, Hanuman has transcended the boundaries of culture and faith, offering solace and guidance to those who seek his presence in their lives.

In these pages, you will not only encounter the epic battles and legendary exploits of the Monkey God but also witness the profound wisdom and teachings that have made him a revered figure in the pantheon of Hindu deities. His life is a testament to the enduring power of faith, the triumph of good over evil, and the unbreakable bond between the mortal and the divine.

May this journey into the world of Hanuman serve as a source of inspiration, strength, and spiritual awakening, reminding us that within each of us lies the potential for boundless devotion and greatness. As we turn the pages of this book, let us, like Hanuman, find the courage to leap over the obstacles in our path and carry the mountain of our burdens with unwavering faith.

In the spirit of devotion and exploration, we invite you to join us in the timeless saga of Hanuman, the Immortal Monkey God.

Birth and Childhood of Lord Hanuman

Long ago, in the celestial realms, there lived a mighty monkey king named Kesari. He was a devoted follower of Lord Shiva and spent his life in penance and worship. Pleased with his devotion, Lord Shiva granted him a divine blessing that his son would be a reincarnation of Lord Shiva himself. Meanwhile, in another realm, there was a celestial nymph named Anjana. She was known for her beauty and purity, but due to a curse, she was born on Earth as a monkey. Anjana, long after she was born on Earth as a monkey due to a cursing for redemption, performed rigorous penance to be blessed with a divine child. Her prayers were answered, and she received a boon from Lord Shiva that she would give birth to a son who possessed extraordinary strength and divine powers.

The combined blessings of Lord Shiva and the celestial deities led to a remarkable event. Anjana and Kesari were married, and soon, Anjana conceived a child who embodied the essence of both Lord Shiva and the divine celestial beings. When Hanuman was born, the entire universe felt his divine presence. As a child, Hanuman was mischievous, playful, and endowed with great strength.

He was known for his pranks, which sometimes caused trouble in the monkey kingdom. One day, Hanuman saw the sun in the sky and, mistaking it for a fruit, leaped into the sky to catch it. His leap took him high into the heavens, where he encountered Rahu, a celestial being.

Rahu, amused by Hanuman's audacity, tried to capture him. Hanuman fought back with all his might, displaying his immense strength. The battle caught the attention of the gods, and they intervened. Lord Indra, the king of the gods, hurled his thunderbolt at Hanuman, striking him on the jaw. The blow was so powerful that it sent Hanuman tumbling back to Earth, unconscious.

Seeing this, Lord Vayu, the god of wind and Hanuman's divine parent, became furious. He withdrew all the air from the world, causing chaos and distress. The gods, realizing their mistake, rushed to appease Lord Vayu. They offered various boons and blessings to Hanuman, including invincibility and the ability to change his size and shape at will.

Hanuman was revived and grew up to become a mighty and devoted monkey warrior. His divine powers and unwavering devotion to Lord Rama, as described in the previous response, played a significant role in the epic Ramayana and in establishing him as a beloved deity in Hinduism. Hanuman's childhood exploits, his divine birth, and his lifelong dedication to his divine master continue to inspire countless devotees to this day.

Lord Hanuman and the Sun

Once upon a time, when Hanuman was a young and mischievous monkey, he lived in the forest with his fellow monkeys. One day, he looked up at the sky and saw a radiant, glowing object. It was the Sun, shining brilliantly in the sky, casting its warm and golden rays upon the Earth.

Curiosity stirred in Hanuman's heart, and he decided to approach the Sun, mistaking it for a delicious fruit. With boundless enthusiasm, he leaped into the sky, higher and higher, trying to catch hold of the Sun. The other animals watched in amazement as Hanuman ascended toward the fiery ball of light.

As Hanuman drew closer to the Sun, the heat and intensity of its rays grew more and more unbearable. Yet, his determination and devotion never wavered. He continued his ascent, undeterred by the scorching heat.

The gods in the heavens observed Hanuman's daring endeavor. They were both impressed by his unwavering devotion and concerned for his safety. To protect him from the Sun's searing heat, the gods summoned the mighty wind god, Vayu, to create a cool and gentle breeze around Hanuman.

With Vayu's divine assistance, Hanuman reached the Sun and attempted to catch it. However, the Sun, realizing Hanuman's intentions, decided to teach him a lesson. The Sun transformed into a massive, blazing ball of fire, expanding its size beyond imagination.

Undeterred, Hanuman grew in size as well, expanding to match the Sun's magnitude. In this epic showdown, Hanuman and the Sun stood face to face, both in their colossal forms, defying the laws of nature.

Witnessing this incredible sight, the gods marveled at Hanuman's boundless devotion and his indomitable spirit. Pleased with his unwavering dedication, the Sun revealed its true form and bestowed Hanuman with a divine blessing. It granted him the ability to change his size at will, making him even more powerful.

Hanuman, humbled and enlightened by the Sun's grace, thanked the Sun for the lesson and returned to the Earth. This experience reinforced his determination to serve a higher purpose, and he later became the devoted disciple of Lord Rama, accompanying him on his epic journey to rescue Sita from the demon king Ravana.

The story of Hanuman and the Sun serves as a testament to Hanuman's unyielding devotion and his willingness to go to any lengths to achieve his goals. It also showcases the divine interventions that often shape the destinies of gods and mortals in Hindu mythology.

Lord Rama and Hanuman's First Meeting

In the ancient city of Ayodhya, there lived a young prince named Rama, the embodiment of dharma (righteousness) and virtue. Rama was the eldest son of King Dasharatha and was adored by all for his impeccable character and exceptional qualities. Little did he know that his life was about to take a divine turn.

Meanwhile, in the dense forests of Kishkindha, Hanuman, the mighty Monkey God, had spent his early years, unaware of his true potential. He was a devoted disciple of Lord Sugriva, the monkey king, and his destiny was intricately woven into the tapestry of Lord Rama's life.

One fateful day, a beautiful and ethereal lady named Sita visited the forest along with her husband, Lord Rama, and his loyal brother, Lakshmana. They had been exiled to the forest for fourteen years, a consequence of a political maneuver.

As Sita wandered deeper into the forest, she spotted a group of playful monkeys. Unbeknownst to her, these monkeys were under the command of Lord Sugriva, who was hiding in the forest to escape his brother Vali's wrath.

Intrigued by the sight of a radiant and unfamiliar lady, Sita handed a precious ornament, a pearl necklace, to Lakshmana and asked him to drop it as a mark of their presence, hoping someone would find it and come to their aid.

The necklace eventually found its way into the hands of Hanuman, who was known for his intelligence and wisdom. When he examined the pearl necklace, he realized that it was a divine sign and an opportunity to serve a higher purpose.

Filled with curiosity and devotion, Hanuman approached Lord Rama, who was residing on the shores of the Pampa Lake. As Hanuman approached the prince, he took on a humble form, shrinking himself to appear as a monkey of ordinary size. Bowing deeply, Hanuman introduced himself and narrated the story of the divine pearl necklace.

Lord Rama, deeply moved by Hanuman's devotion and the story of Sita's plight, recognized the Monkey God's extraordinary nature. He sensed that Hanuman would play a crucial role in their future endeavors.

In return for his service, Lord Rama lovingly embraced Hanuman, and their hearts connected in an unspoken bond of trust and devotion. Rama felt an immediate affection for Hanuman, recognizing his selflessness and courage.

This moment marked the beginning of a profound relationship between Lord Rama and Hanuman. Hanuman pledged his unwavering loyalty to Rama, and from that day forward, he became an indispensable part of Rama's journey, offering his strength, wisdom, and devotion to help Rama in his quest to rescue Sita and fulfill his divine purpose.

The first meeting of Lord Rama and Hanuman symbolizes the union of unwavering devotion and divine purpose, setting the stage for the legendary adventures and trials they would face together in their pursuit of righteousness and dharma.

Devotion to Lord Rama and the Search for Sita:

Hanuman's devotion to Lord Rama was unparalleled. He considered Lord Rama not only as his master but also as his very reason for existence. When Lord Rama, along with his wife Sita and his loyal brother

Lakshmana, was living in the forest during his exile, Hanuman's life was intertwined with theirs.

One day, while Sita was alone in their forest hermitage, the demon king Ravana, who coveted her beauty, disguised himself as a beggar and cunningly kidnapped her. Sita was held captive in Ravana's magnificent palace in Lanka (modern-day Sri Lanka). When Lord Rama and Lakshmana returned to their hermitage and found Sita missing, they were devastated. Lord Rama was determined to rescue his beloved wife, and he had the support of a formidable army of monkeys, bears, and other divine beings.

Among this army, Hanuman stood out not only because of his incredible strength but also due to his unwavering devotion to Lord Rama. He was chosen to be the messenger to reach Lanka, locate Sita, and convey Lord Rama's message to her. With a mighty leap, Hanuman soared across the ocean and landed in Lanka. He assumed a small form to remain unnoticed and began his search for Sita. After many trials and tribulations, Hanuman finally found her in the Ashoka

Vatika, where she was kept captive and heartbroken. Hanuman approached Sita and reassured her by chanting Lord Rama's name and showing her his ring, which had Lord Rama's image. Sita was overjoyed to see Hanuman and received his message of hope and rescue. Hanuman's devotion and unwavering faith in Lord Rama moved Sita deeply. She provided Hanuman with a message for Lord Rama, along with a hairpin as a token to prove her identity. With this newfound hope and determination, Hanuman prepared to return to Lord Rama and share the news of Sita's location. However, before leaving Lanka, Hanuman decided to teach Ravana and his army a lesson they would never forget. He set fire to Lanka with his fiery tail, causing chaos and destruction. This act not only displayed his immense power but also symbolized his fierce devotion to Lord Rama.

After completing his mission, Hanuman made his way back to Lord Rama and shared the news of Sita's whereabouts. His dedication, intelligence, and bravery made him an invaluable asset in the subsequent war against Ravana and his forces.

Hanuman's devotion to Lord Rama remains a symbol of unwavering faith and selfless service. His role in the search for Sita and the eventual rescue mission is celebrated in Hindu texts and is a testament to his extraordinary love and loyalty to his divine master.

The Leap to Lanka:

After discovering Sita's location in Lanka, Hanuman faced the daunting task of returning to Lord Rama and sharing this critical information with him. The vast expanse of the ocean lay before him, separating the southern tip of India from Lanka, which is modern-day Sri Lanka. Hanuman knew that he had to cross this massive obstacle to fulfill his mission.

Hanuman stood at the shores of the Indian Ocean, his massive form radiating with divine energy. His devotion to Lord Rama was unwavering, and he had faith that with Lord Rama's name on his lips, he could accomplish any feat. He folded his hands in prayer to Lord Rama, seeking his blessings for this extraordinary endeavor.

With a mighty roar of "Jai Shri Ram!" (Hail Lord Rama), Hanuman took a deep breath and crouched low. His powerful legs tensed, and then, with an explosive burst of energy, he leaped into the sky. The ground shook beneath him, and the trees swayed as Hanuman soared upwards.

Higher and higher he went, his vision encompassing the entire subcontinent below. The gods and celestial beings watched in awe as Hanuman defied the laws of nature. His form was a blur as he propelled himself across the ocean with astonishing speed.

The creatures of the sea, including the massive sea serpents, were astounded by the sight of this mighty monkey flying over the water. Even the ocean itself seemed to rise to greet him, its waves parting to make way for the devoted messenger of Lord Rama.

As Hanuman crossed the ocean, he encountered a series of trials and tribulations, including the attempts of a sea demoness named Surasa to capture him. However, Hanuman's devotion and determination were unwavering, and he overcame each challenge with grace and skill.

Finally, after a breathtaking journey that defied description, Hanuman spotted the shores of Lanka in the distance. With another powerful leap, he descended upon Lanka like a thunderbolt, causing the earth to tremble upon his arrival.

Hanuman had successfully completed his incredible leap and had reached the land where Sita was held captive. He knew that this was just the beginning of his mission to rescue Sita and reunite her with Lord Rama. His heroic act of leaping across the ocean had not only showcased his physical strength but also symbolized the limitless power of devotion and the lengths to which one would go to serve and protect their beloved Lord.

With unwavering determination, Hanuman continued his quest to find Sita and bring her back to Lord Rama, demonstrating his extraordinary devotion and unwavering commitment to his divine master.

Meeting Sita:

In the heart of Lanka, the once-lustrous Ashoka Vatika had lost its charm, shrouded in darkness and despair. Sita, the virtuous wife of Lord Rama, sat beneath a magnificent tree, her radiant beauty marred by tears and sorrow. Her spirit remained unbroken, but her captivity had taken its toll.

As the moon cast its silver light upon the garden, a shadow fell upon Sita. She looked up, her eyes searching for the source of this unexpected intrusion. What she saw, however, was beyond her imagination.

A colossal figure descended from the heavens, landing gracefully before her. It was Hanuman, the mighty monkey god, whose divine form radiated with a gentle yet awe-inspiring aura. His eyes held a compassionate light, and his presence, though monumental, exuded an air of humility.

Sita, initially cautious, observed Hanuman with a mix of curiosity and hope. His countenance reassured her, and she sensed that he was not an ordinary visitor. Hanuman knelt before Sita, his voice soothing like the gentlest of breezes.

"Devi," he began, "I am Hanuman, a humble servant of Lord Rama. I come with tidings of hope and deliverance."

Sita's heart skipped a beat at the mention of her beloved husband's name. Her eyes glistened with newfound hope as she listened intently to Hanuman's words.

Hanuman spoke of Lord Rama's unshakeable love for her, his relentless search, and his vow to rescue her from Ravana's clutches. With each word, Sita's heart swelled with a mixture of joy and longing. She yearned to see her husband, to be cradled in his strong arms, and to feel the warmth of his love once more.

To dispel any doubt and strengthen Sita's faith, Hanuman extended his open palm, revealing a precious token—a magnificent ring adorned with Lord Rama's image. Sita recognized it immediately, for it was a symbol of their sacred bond.

Overwhelmed with emotion, Sita gently placed her hand on the ring, her fingers trembling with gratitude and love. Tears flowed freely down her cheeks as she clutched the cherished memento to her heart.

"Devi," Hanuman said softly, "I am here to assure you that Lord Rama is well aware of your suffering. He carries you in his heart, and his love for you is boundless. You need not fear, for your days of captivity are numbered."

Sita's eyes met Hanuman's, and in that moment, a profound connection was forged between them. She spoke with a voice filled with love, faith, and longing, urging Hanuman to reassure Lord Rama of her unwavering devotion and her eagerness to be reunited with him.

With a heart full of gratitude and renewed hope, Sita bestowed her blessings upon Hanuman and prayed for his safety and success in the mission to rescue her. Hanuman, touched by her resilience and purity, bowed respectfully before her and prepared to return to Lord Rama.

As he ascended into the heavens, Sita's gaze lingered on the departing figure of Hanuman. With tears of gratitude in her eyes, she knew that her message of love and faith would reach Lord Rama, igniting the flames of hope in his heart and inspiring their inevitable reunion. In that sacred encounter beneath the moonlight, Hanuman had brought solace and hope to Sita, reaffirming her unwavering love and faith in Lord Rama, and marking a poignant moment in the timeless epic of the Ravan.

Burning Lanka:

The moonlight bathed Lanka in its silvery glow, casting long shadows over the city. The once-great kingdom, ruled by the demon king Ravana, lay in a deceptive calm, unaware of the impending storm.

Amidst the quietude, Hanuman, the mighty monkey god and devoted disciple of Lord Rama, stood poised on the rooftop of a towering palace. His massive form was outlined against the night sky, his tail crackling with flames like a comet's tail. Hanuman's eyes blazed with determination, and his heart beat in rhythm with the name of his beloved Lord Rama.

He knew that Sita, the virtuous wife of Lord Rama, was imprisoned somewhere in this city, suffering in captivity. His mission was to locate her and deliver Lord Rama's message of hope and rescue. But he also understood that his mere presence in Lanka would not remain unnoticed for long.

With a resounding roar that echoed through the city, Hanuman's fiery tail ignited, casting a blazing trail across the dark sky. The flames danced like serpents as he directed their fury towards the city below. The very air seemed to catch fire, and the heavens themselves bore witness to this celestial display of power and devotion.

The city of Lanka was caught off guard. Panic and chaos erupted as flames engulfed homes, palaces, and streets. Ravana's demon warriors rushed to extinguish the inferno, but their efforts were in vain. Hanuman's fiery tail was a force of nature, unrelenting and unstoppable.

The cries of demons and the crackling of flames filled the night, and the once-majestic city began to crumble under the relentless assault of fire. Even the demon king Ravana himself, watching from his towering palace, was shaken by the magnitude of the destruction.

Amidst the chaos, Hanuman maintained his focus, his heart unwavering in its devotion to Lord Rama. He knew that his act was a demonstration of his love and loyalty to his master, and it was a message to the world that nothing could stand in the way of Lord Rama's divine mission.

As the flames continued to rage, Hanuman completed his mission. He located Sita in the Ashoka Vatika and delivered Lord Rama's message of hope and love. Sita, surrounded by the destruction caused by Hanuman's fiery tail, found solace in his presence and the assurance that Lord Rama was coming to rescue her.

Having accomplished his task, Hanuman retracted his fiery tail and stood on the rooftop, his form now bathed in the soft moonlight once more. The city of Lanka lay in ruins, a testament to the power of devotion and the unwavering commitment of a devoted servant to his beloved Lord.

With the memory of Sita's grateful smile in his heart, Hanuman spread his wings and leaped back into the night sky. His return to Lord Rama was imminent, and his act of valor and devotion had further solidified his reputation as a divine being, a symbol of unwavering faith and selfless service for generations to come.

The War against Ravana:

The battleground was set, and the tension hung in the air like a storm about to break. Lord Rama, accompanied by his loyal army of monkeys, bears, and divine beings, stood on the shores of Lanka, ready to confront the formidable forces of the demon king Ravana. The war for Sita's liberation had begun, and Hanuman, the embodiment of devotion and strength, was at the forefront.

As the war drums resonated, Hanuman took his position with an air of quiet determination. His eyes gleamed with the fire of purpose, and his muscular frame radiated with divine energy. He knew that the battles ahead would test not only his physical prowess but also his intellect and strategic acumen.

Ravana, seated upon his fearsome chariot, led the demon army, a formidable force that appeared endless. His generals, including the mighty warriors Indrajit and Kumbhakarna, were equally fierce and determined to protect their king.

The battle began with a deafening clash of swords and a volley of arrows that darkened the sky. Hanuman soared into the heart of the enemy's ranks, his very presence striking fear into the demon warriors. With a mighty roar, he unleashed his unparalleled strength, pummeling the enemy with punches that sent demons flying in all directions.

Indrajit, known for his mastery of magic and warfare, attempted to ensnare Hanuman in a web of illusion. But Hanuman's intellect was as sharp as his brawn. With a knowing smile, he used his divine vision to see through the illusions and swiftly defeated Indrajit, shattering his magical defenses.

Kumbhakarna, the colossal demon with an insatiable appetite, was awakened to join the battle. His immense size and strength posed a daunting challenge. However, Hanuman, undaunted, used his agility to evade Kumbhakarna's devastating blows, eventually wearing down the demon with a relentless assault of punches.

But it wasn't just physical prowess that made Hanuman a formidable warrior. His strategic brilliance was on full display. He devised clever tactics to outmaneuver the demon forces, creating diversions, and leading them into traps set by Lord Rama's army. His ability to analyze battlefield situations and adapt quickly was a testament to his intellect.

The war raged on for days, with Hanuman at the heart of every crucial battle. His unwavering loyalty to Lord Rama and his fearlessness on the battlefield inspired the monkey and bear warriors, driving them to achieve remarkable feats of valor.

As the war approached its climax, Hanuman's moment of ultimate heroism arrived. Ravana, the demon king himself, stepped onto the battlefield, wielding his mighty sword and displaying his dark powers. It was a duel of epic proportions, and the fate of Lanka hung in the balance.

Hanuman and Ravana clashed in a fierce battle, their blows echoing like thunder across the battlefield. Hanuman's strength and devotion, however, proved to be more powerful than any dark magic. With a final, earth-shattering blow, Hanuman defeated Ravana, bringing an end to the demon king's tyranny.

The war against Ravana was a triumph of righteousness and devotion, with Hanuman's indomitable spirit and unmatched strength playing a pivotal role in the victory. Sita was finally rescued from her captivity, and Lord Rama's dharma (duty) was fulfilled.

Hanuman's heroic deeds in the war were celebrated for generations to come, solidifying his status as a symbol of unwavering devotion, boundless strength, and divine grace. His role in the epic battle was a testament to his commitment to his beloved Lord Rama and the triumph of good over evil.

Bringing the Sanjivani Herb:

The battlefield was fraught with tension as the war between Lord Rama's army and Ravana's demon forces raged on. The clash of swords, the thunder of chariots, and the cries of warriors filled the air. Amidst this chaos, a moment of despair struck like a bolt of lightning.

Lakshmana, Lord Rama's valiant brother, lay wounded and unconscious on the battlefield. A powerful arrow, infused with dark magic, had struck him down, leaving no hope for his survival. Lord Rama's anguish was palpable as he cradled Lakshmana's lifeless form in his arms, tears streaming down his face.

The sages and physicians present on the battlefield recognized the gravity of the situation. They knew that the only remedy for Lakshmana's life-threatening injuries was the elusive Sanjivani herb—a miraculous herb capable of reviving the dead and healing the gravest wounds. However, this miraculous herb grew exclusively in the distant Dronagiri Mountains, located far to the north.

With no time to spare, Lord Rama turned to Hanuman, the embodiment of strength and devotion. He beseeched Hanuman to embark on a perilous mission to retrieve the life-saving Sanjivani herb and save Lakshmana's life.

Hanuman's eyes filled with determination as he bowed before Lord Rama. He accepted the divine responsibility without hesitation, fully aware of the immense distance and treacherous terrain that lay ahead.

With a mighty leap, Hanuman soared into the sky, leaving behind a trail of stardust. The very heavens marveled at his speed and determination as he headed north, in the direction of the Dronagiri Mountains.

The journey was fraught with challenges. Hanuman crossed vast rivers, scaled towering peaks, and battled fierce winds. He remained undeterred by the obstacles that tested his strength and resolve.

Finally, after what seemed like an eternity, Hanuman reached the Dronagiri Mountains. However, the Sanjivani herb was not easily distinguishable. It was hidden among countless other herbs, and Hanuman couldn't afford to make a mistake.

In his desperation to save Lakshmana, Hanuman decided on a daring plan. He uprooted the entire Dronagiri Mountain itself, holding it aloft with his mighty shoulders. The sheer force of his strength and devotion astounded the gods and sages watching from above.

With the colossal mountain in his grasp, Hanuman soared back towards the battlefield. His flight was a spectacle that defied nature, with the mountain held high above him like a divine umbrella.

As Hanuman descended upon the battlefield, the sages and physicians quickly identified the Sanjivani herb within the mountain. They carefully plucked the life-saving herb, and with Lord Rama's blessings, applied it to Lakshmana's wounds.

Miraculously, Lakshmana's life force was revived. Color returned to his cheeks, and his eyes flickered open, filled with gratitude and relief. Lord Rama's face lit up with joy as he embraced his beloved brother, tears of gratitude streaming down his cheeks.

The mission to retrieve the Sanjivani herb had been a testament to Hanuman's unwavering devotion and boundless strength. His heroic act not only saved Lakshmana's life but also demonstrated the power of love and devotion in the face of seemingly insurmountable challenges.

As Hanuman's flight back to the battlefield was celebrated with cheers and hymns of praise, his name became synonymous with courage, devotion, and selfless service—a beacon of hope for all who faced adversity.

After the War:

With the defeat of Ravana and the rescue of Sita, Lanka's dark reign came to an end. The battlefield bore the scars of a great war, but the victory of righteousness had been won. Lord Rama's unwavering dedication and the valor of his army had triumphed over the forces of evil.

Amidst the jubilation, one figure stood out—the mighty Hanuman, whose strength, devotion, and courage had been instrumental in Lord Rama's victory. His eyes shone with pride as he knelt before Lord Rama, his heart filled with gratitude and humility.

Lord Rama, recognizing Hanuman's extraordinary service and undying loyalty, embraced him with deep affection. He spoke words of admiration and love, declaring Hanuman to be the embodiment of devotion, strength, and selfless service. It was a moment of profound bonding between master and disciple, a testament to their unbreakable connection.

As the days passed, Lord Rama, along with his beloved wife Sita and faithful brother Lakshmana, prepared to return to Ayodhya. Hanuman, the devoted guardian and servant, accompanied them on their journey. His role in the epic Ramayana was not just that of a warrior but also a symbol of unwavering devotion and selflessness.

Upon reaching Ayodhya, Lord Rama was crowned as the rightful king, and the kingdom celebrated their return with unparalleled joy. Hanuman, however, remained ever watchful, ready to fulfill his duties at a moment's notice.

Lord Rama's admiration for Hanuman knew no bounds. He declared to his subjects that those who worshipped Hanuman with sincerity and devotion would receive his blessings. Hanuman became a beloved deity, revered not only for his physical strength but also for his spiritual power and grace.

In Ayodhya, Hanuman's presence was felt in every corner of the kingdom. Devotees built temples in his honor, where his image was enshrined, and hymns of his valor and devotion were sung with reverence. People from all walks of life sought his blessings for courage, strength, and unwavering faith.

Hanuman's fame transcended the boundaries of Ayodhya, spreading far and wide. His story became an enduring symbol of devotion, a reminder that with faith and determination, one could overcome the most formidable obstacles. He was celebrated not only as a divine being but also as an inspiration for humanity.

As Hanuman continued to serve Lord Rama faithfully, his legacy grew with each passing generation. His teachings of devotion, humility, and selfless service remained etched in the hearts of millions. Hanuman had not only fulfilled his role as a warrior but had also become a spiritual guide and a source of boundless inspiration for all who sought the path of righteousness and devotion.

Immortality:

In the heart of devotion and the depths of unwavering faith, the story of Hanuman transcends time and space, weaving itself into the fabric of spirituality and culture. Hanuman, the monkey-faced deity, embodies the very essence of devotion, making him a beloved and immortal figure in Hinduism.

As the ages passed, Hanuman's legend only grew in magnitude. His story was not just a tale from ancient scriptures but a living, breathing inspiration for generations to come. His devotion to Lord Rama and his selfless service during the epic Ramayana had left an indelible mark on the hearts of millions.

Devotees sought solace and strength in his name, turning to the Hanuman Chalisa and the Hanuman Ashtak as profound expressions of their reverence. These sacred texts, composed in praise of Hanuman, became vessels of devotion, carrying the hopes, dreams, and prayers of countless souls to the divine.

Hanuman's image, often depicted as a monkey-faced deity with a muscular frame, became an iconic symbol of courage and unwavering faith. His very presence was a reminder that no obstacle was insurmountable for those who carried the flame of devotion within their hearts.

Each year, millions of devotees flocked to temples dedicated to Hanuman, seeking his blessings and guidance. His presence was felt not only in places of worship but also in the hearts of those who faced adversity with courage, knowing that Hanuman's strength was with them.

Hanuman's teachings transcended religious boundaries, emphasizing values that resonated with people from all walks of life. His devotion to Lord Rama served as a universal reminder of the power of faith and the boundless potential of the human spirit.

In the tapestry of time, Hanuman's story remained evergreen, a testament to the enduring power of devotion, the strength of unwavering faith, and the significance of selfless service. His immortality was not limited to the pages of ancient texts; it lived on in the hearts and souls of those who found inspiration in his story.

The story of Hanuman, the monkey-faced deity, served as a beacon of hope, reminding humanity that in the face of life's trials and tribulations, one could always turn to the immortal spirit of devotion for guidance, strength, and solace.